EXPLORING ARTIFICIAL INTELLIGENCE

THE CHALLENGES OF AI

Lisa Idzikowski

Lerner Publications ◆ Minneapolis

For my family

Lerner Publications Company
An imprint of Lerner Publishing Group, Inc.
241 First Avenue North
Minneapolis, MN 55401 USA

For reading levels and more information, look up this title at www.lernerbooks.com.

Main body text set in Aptifer Sans LT Pro.
Typeface provided by Linotype AG.

Editor: Nicole Berglund **Designer:** Viet Chu **Photo Editor:** Nicole Berglund
Lerner team: Martha Kranes

Library of Congress Cataloging-in-Publication Data

Names: Idzikowski, Lisa, author.
Title: The challenges of AI / Lisa Idzikowski.
Description: Minneapolis : Lerner Publications, [2025] | Series: Exploring artificial intelligence | Includes bibliographical references and index. | Audience: Ages 8–12 | Audience: Grades 4–6 | Summary: "AI is an exciting technology that continues to improve. But it's not without its challenges. Readers learn about the issues of AI, from taking human jobs to spreading misinformation"— Provided by publisher.
Identifiers: LCCN 2024013880 (print) | LCCN 2024013881 (ebook) | ISBN 9798765647899 (library binding) | ISBN 9798765661666 (pbk.) | ISBN 9798765654514 (epub)
Subjects: LCSH: Artificial intelligence—Juvenile literature.
Classification: LCC Q335.4 .I388 2025 (print) | LCC Q335.4 (ebook) | DDC 006.3—dc23/eng/20240628

LC record available at https://lccn.loc.gov/2024013880
LC ebook record available at https://lccn.loc.gov/2024013881

Manufactured in the United States of America
1-1011014-53350-8/6/2024

TABLE OF CONTENTS

INTRODUCTION

LOOK CLOSELY

President Kennedy talks to Congress in 1961.

On May 25, 1961, then US president John F. Kennedy spoke to Congress. The president said that the United States should have a goal to put a human on the moon and bring them back to Earth safely. His speech sparked people's imaginations. Scientists, engineers, schoolkids, and parents joined in the excitement.

It took eight years, but at almost eleven o'clock at night eastern time, July 20, 1969, Neil Armstrong of the Apollo 11 mission stepped out of his spacecraft and down onto the moon. As many as six hundred million people on Earth watched on TV. The crew ran experiments, collected samples, and left. Four days later, the astronauts splashed down into the Pacific Ocean. They were safely back on Earth.

Astronauts Buzz Aldrin (*above*) and Neil Armstrong left an American flag on the moon during the Apollo 11 mission.

But what if TV reports said otherwise? What if the news claimed the astronauts had died on the moon? How could someone know the truth? Artificial intelligence (AI) software makes it possible to create fake videos. These can show people doing or saying things they never did in real life. Made-up videos, photos, and sound recordings are called deepfakes.

Neil Armstrong (*front*) prepares to leave on the Apollo 11 mission.

MIT's moon landing deepfake is played at an exhibit in 2024.

In 2020 the Massachusetts Institute of Technology (MIT) made a deepfake video about the Apollo 11 moon landing. The video shows then president Richard Nixon claiming the astronauts had died on the moon. The deepfake proved how convincing fake videos and misinformation can seem. The video's producers hope people will remember this deepfake in the future and question whether what they view is real or fake. AI and deep learning made the deepfake possible.

College students study in a library in the 1950s.

CHAPTER 1
WHAT A DAY!

What did people do before computers, the internet, or AI? People watched more movies on a big screen at a theater. Students found information in encyclopedias at libraries for their homework. More people wrote letters to friends and relatives using paper and pen. No one had cell phones to carry with them, so they used landline phones or phone booths. Engineers, scientists, and students used a special handheld tool called a slide rule to solve math problems. NASA scientists even used them to build rockets and plan the Apollo 11 moon mission!

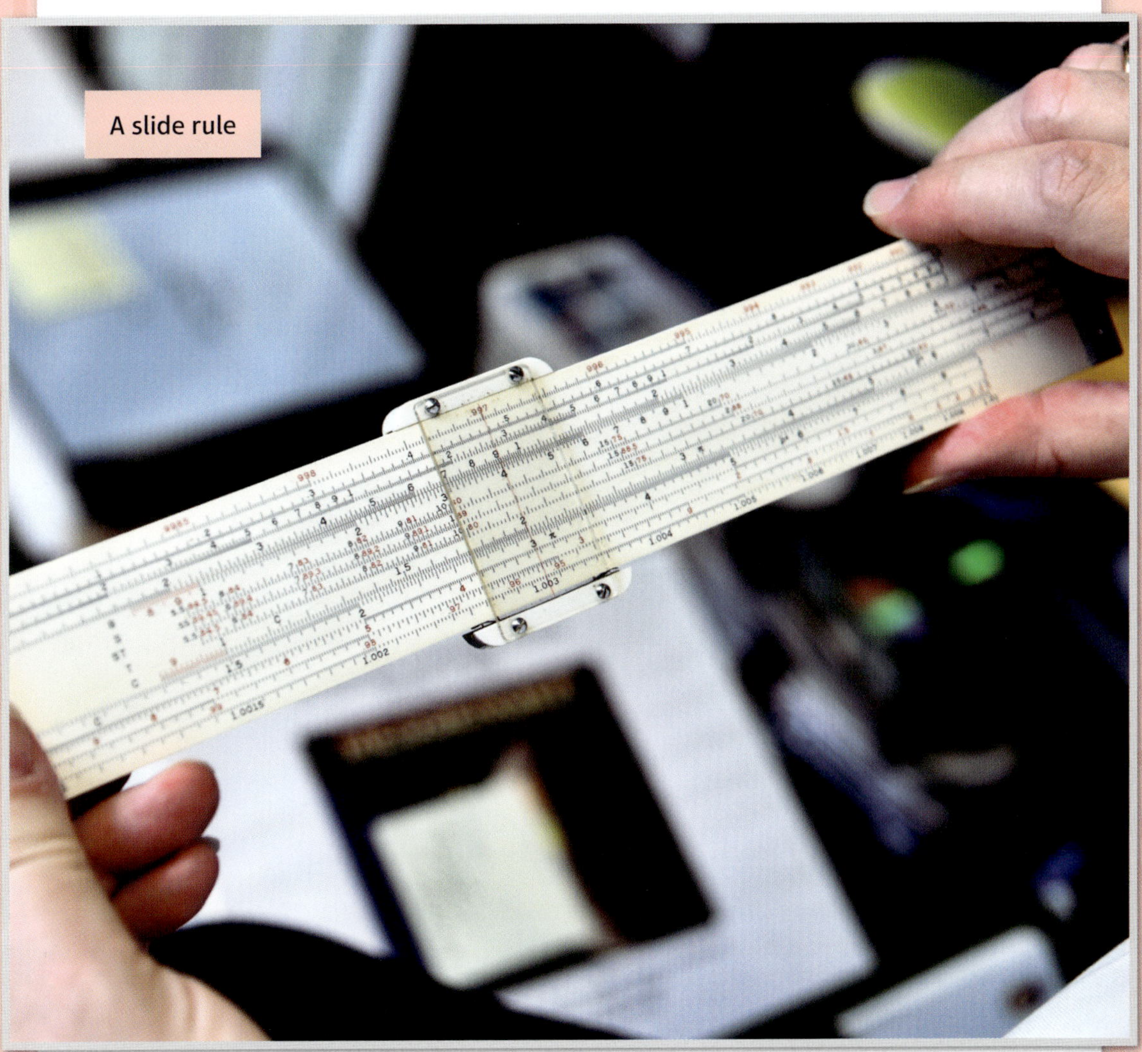

A slide rule

Slide rules worked well. But engineers and scientists wanted to solve problems faster. The Electronic Numerical Integrator and Computer (ENIAC), the first electronic computer, was completed in 1946. Newspapers called early computers magic brains or wonder brains. People thought these computers were amazing and could think like a human being.

Workers operate the ENIAC.

Engineers and scientists improved computers. They wanted machines that could learn, talk, write, and read. AI made that possible. Computer scientists thought these new AI-powered computers were incredible. Some scientists even argued that the AI computers would have a bigger impact than electricity! Even though these machine systems appeared intelligent, they posed challenges too.

At School

ChatGPT first came out in 2022. It is a generative AI tool, meaning it is able to generate text, images, videos, and other things in response to a prompt. Some schools teach students how to use ChatGPT due to how useful it can be. Students can practice multiplication with ChatGPT. They can also learn about computer science.

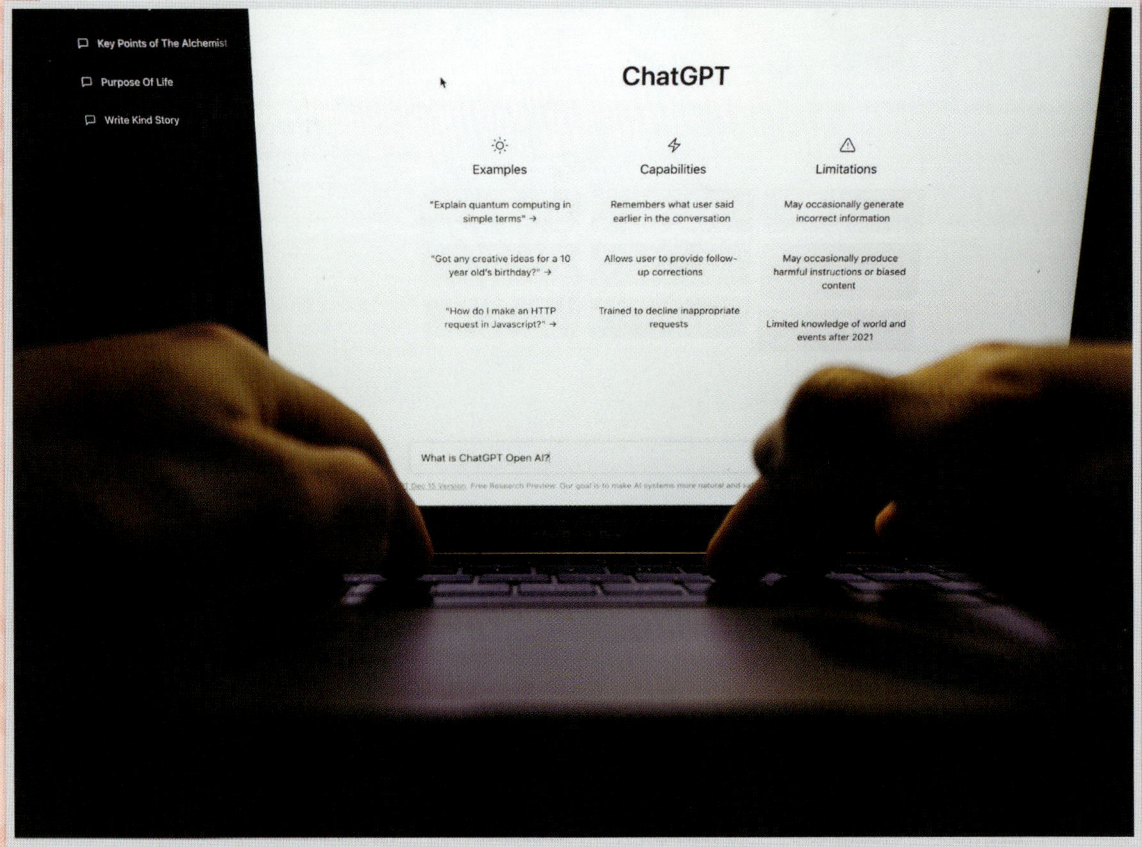

OpenAI, the creator of ChatGPT, was cofounded by Elon Musk, the CEO of Tesla.

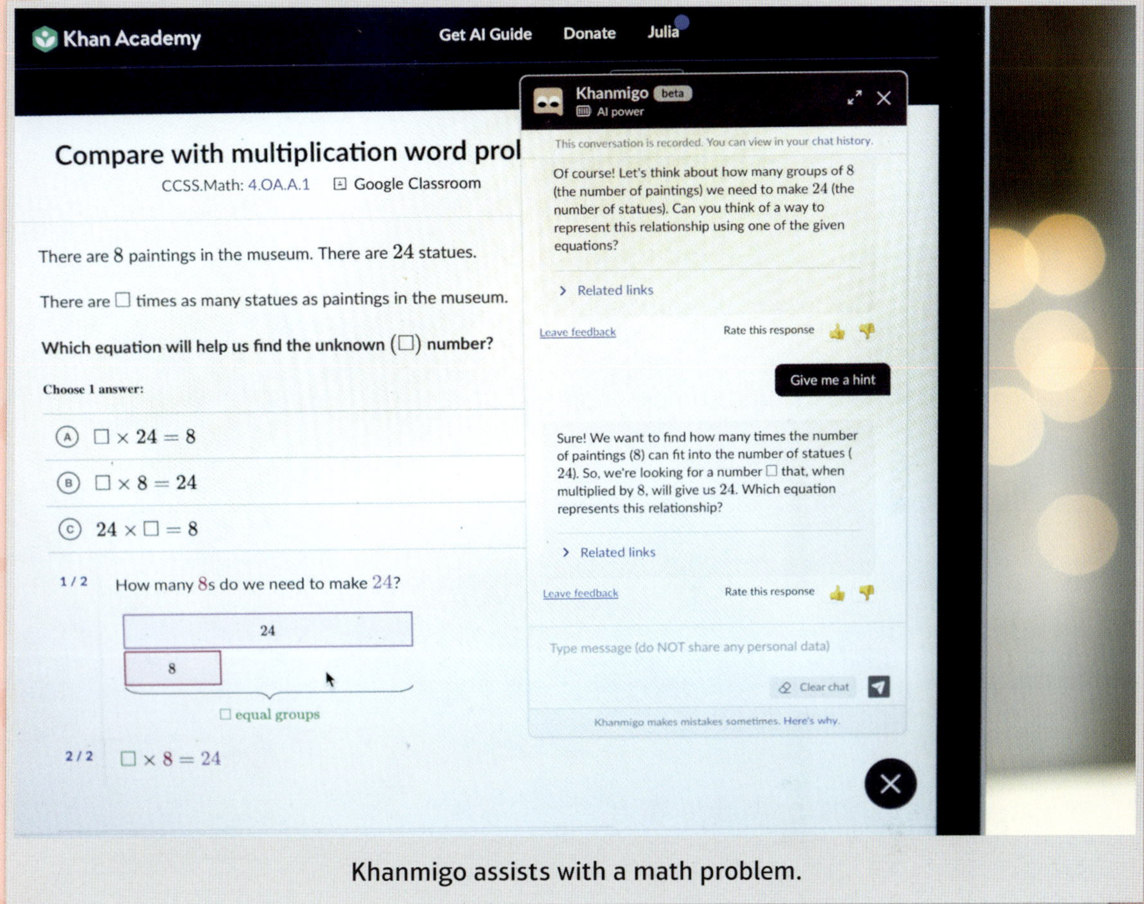

Khanmigo assists with a math problem.

Students can even learn in other languages with chatbots. Khanmigo is a chatbot tutor that speaks in multiple languages. It guides students to answers as they learn. It won't just give an answer or do the work. It teaches. Some kids struggle to pay attention. Khanmigo makes it easier by having someone like Benjamin Franklin or even Winnie the Pooh teach lessons.

Chatbots sound like great tutors. But teachers and parents worry that students will use ChatGPT to cheat. Will students learn to write if AI does it for them? ChatGPT also makes mistakes, and even makes up facts. It could be very hard for a student to tell what is fact and what is made up.

AI Hallucinations

Generative AI models such as ChatGPT, Gemini, or Midjourney can produce wrong information or images. This is called an AI hallucination. These large systems process huge amounts of data while they are in training. If the data put into the systems is wrong, the models can then make mistakes. In 2023 Bard, now called Gemini, said the James Webb Space Telescope took the first picture of a planet outside the solar system. But the first picture of this kind was taken in 2004, long before the Webb telescope even launched.

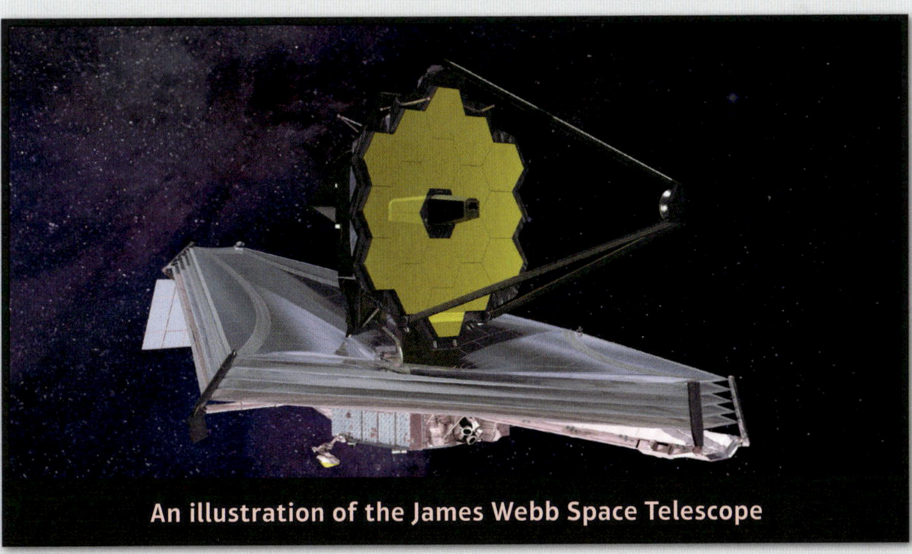

An illustration of the James Webb Space Telescope

Disappearing Jobs

How many jobs will disappear because of AI? It's hard to say. Some jobs are gone already. In 2023 Duolingo, a company that creates language-learning games, replaced 10 percent of its human translators with AI. This helped the company save money, but many wondered if the language lessons would be as good without humans.

In 2024 Duolingo offered courses to learn 40 different languages.

Robots have taken some human jobs assembling cars in factories.

ChatGPT writes computer code. Will computer programmers still be needed? No one knows for sure. But many jobs will stay. What if a toilet backs up? Or a light doesn't work? AI cannot fix things as a plumber or electrician can. AI will also create new jobs. Machine learning systems need special engineers and data scientists to keep them working correctly.

CHAPTER 2

THAT CAN'T BE REAL

There is so much stuff to buy online and in person. How do you decide what to buy? Companies use celebrities in their ads to sell products. You might see musician Taylor Swift wearing a certain pair of jeans. Or retired football player Tom Brady wearing the latest sneakers. But is everything in these ads true? Look closely next time you see a celebrity in an ad. It might be a deepfake.

Deep learning networks are fed lots of pictures. The system then mixes things up. It manipulates real images into fake ones. Someone's face might be put on another person's body. Someone's voice could come out of another person's mouth. Deepfakes can show a person doing or saying something totally untrue.

The term *deepfake* was first used in 2017.

DAVID BECKHAM

Malaria is a disease found mainly in tropical areas. People get the disease when an infected mosquito bites them. Technology is helping with the worldwide effort to stop this disease. Soccer star David Beckham teamed up with a tech company to make an ad using AI technology to help draw attention to the disease. In the synthetic video, Beckham seems to speak in nine different languages while promoting the fight against malaria. Beckham doesn't speak all these languages in real life.

David Beckham

Fun or Fearful?

Are deepfakes fun or fearful? In 2023 an image of Pope Francis, the head of the Catholic Church, wearing a white puffer coat spread online. Many people on social media questioned the photo. It turned out to be a picture made by AI. Social media has also shown deepfakes of important people, such as presidents, being arrested or jailed. Deepfake videos of presidents saying misleading things have spread online too. Generative AI tools Midjourney and Dall-E can create these fakes.

This 2023 deepfake of Pope Francis was created using Midjourney.

Researchers first thought about deepfakes in the 1990s, though the technology was developed in the 2010s.

Spotting Fakes

There is good and bad news about spotting a deepfake. The bad news is that it's hard. Researchers are trying to build systems to spot fakes. But people can also try to find them. Look at faces closely. Is the skin too smooth or too wrinkly? Does the hair seem real? Is the person blinking too much or too little? There is also good news. AI systems are getting better at finding fakes. And people can get better at it too.

CHAPTER 3

DOES AI CARE?

AI can do many things well. It can solve math problems superfast. It can help with homework. It can control self-driving cars. But can AI care about people? One computer scientist said computers should not replace human understanding. Humans care about one another. Trust is important too. Communities work best when people care about and trust one another. Human brains are naturally built to trust others.

AI That Cares

Eliza, a chatbot from 1966, seemed to care about people. People fed scripts into the machine's program. An algorithm made the system act like a therapist. Several years later, another chatbot was created. Parry was programmed to act how psychiatrists at the time thought a patient with a mental illness would act. Parry's creator hoped the system

Joseph Weizenbaum, a professor and computer scientist, invented the chatbot Eliza.

would help psychiatric research and help psychiatrists learn about patients. Parry could respond to certain prompts with preprogrammed answers.

Modern chatbots provide therapy. Some people prefer talking to them instead of a person. But doctors question these services. Some say there's no proof that machine therapists work.

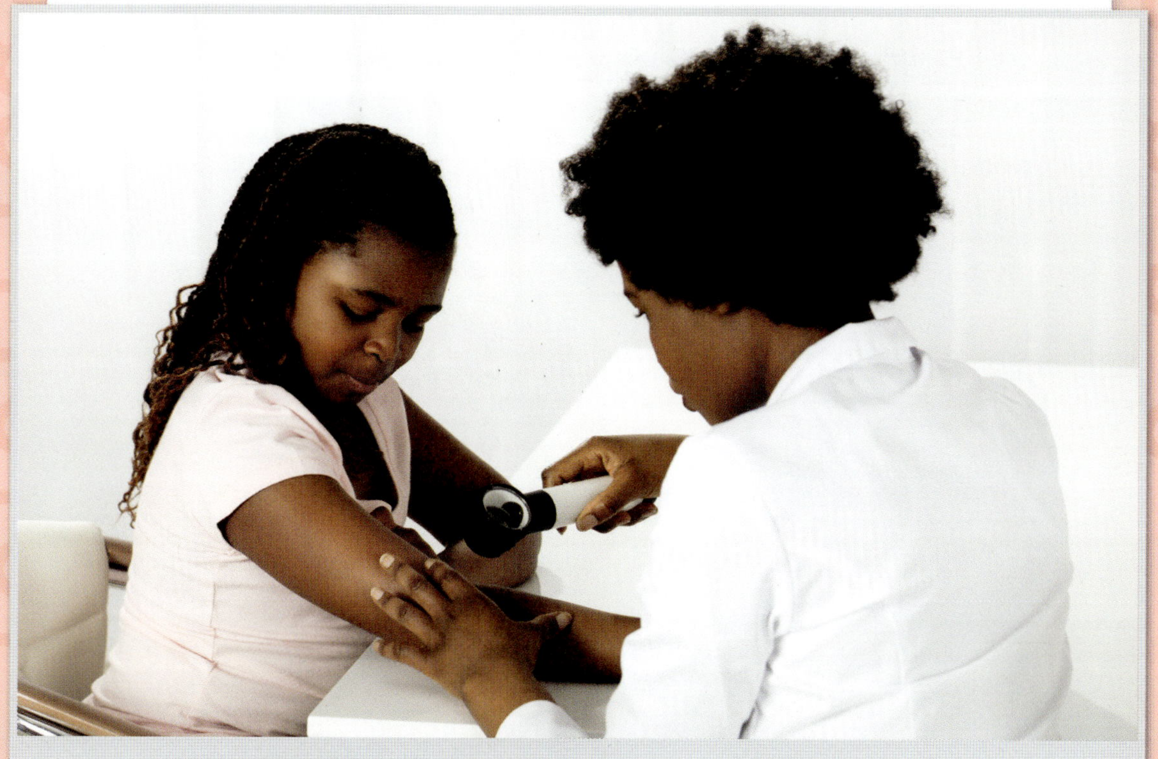

Doctors that treat skin issues are called dermatologists.

Fair or Good

Without a doubt, AI helps people in many ways. But can AI systems be fair? AI systems display bias because of the data they are trained on. Bias is a prejudice for or against someone or something. It is based on opinion instead of fact and can be harmful and unfair.

AI bias can be very dangerous. Bias is seen in AI that helps spot skin cancer. The systems cannot always spot skin cancer on darker skin. They are trained to spot skin cancer on lighter skin. AI is also best at recognizing the faces of white men and has trouble identifying the faces of older adults and darker-skinned people. This can cause issues in law enforcement. Police might use AI to scan security footage of a criminal. The AI has not been trained on many faces, so it may have trouble identifying the correct person in the footage.

A police officer shows how AI is used to recognize faces and help solve crimes.

What a Dog!

Dogs give love and comfort to their owners. Some people may want to have a dog, but they can't do all the feeding, walking, and cleaning that a dog needs. A robot dog may be the answer! AI powers these machines. Aibo, a robotic dog, barks, wags its tail, does tricks, and has big eyes that blink. Aibo even uses AI to develop its own personality! It might be the perfect pet.

Sony released the first model of Aibo in 1999.

President Biden (*center*) hosted a meeting with AI experts in 2023 to work on keeping AI safe.

AI is all around us in our everyday lives. It is helpful in many ways. But it poses challenges. AI experts, governments, and people from all walks of life agree that care must be taken with AI now and in the future.

Glossary

AI hallucination: incorrect or false information produced by an AI system

artificial intelligence (AI): technology that makes computers and machines seem to think like humans

bias: prejudice for or against someone or something

chatbot: any software simulating human conversation with a person

deepfake: videos, images, and sound recordings that have been manipulated to show events that never occurred or people saying things they never said

deep learning: a form of machine learning

generative AI: a type of AI that produces something new such as text, images, videos, or music

machine learning: the way a machine learns without being programmed to do so

prejudice: an unfair feeling of dislike for a person or group because of race, gender, religion, or something else

synthetic video: a type of video made with AI

Learn More

Britannica Kids: Artificial Intelligence
https://kids.britannica.com/kids/article/artificial-intelligence/390648

Dickmann, Nancy. *Artificial Intelligence*. Tucson, AZ: Brown Bear Books, 2025.

Idzikowski, Lisa. *How AI Works*. Minneapolis: Lerner Publications, 2025.

Kiddle: Chatterbot Facts for Kids
https://kids.kiddle.co/Chatterbot

MacCarald, Clara. *Humans vs. Artificial Intelligence*. Lake Elmo, MN: Focus Readers, 2020.

National Geographic Kids: Could a Robot Become President?
https://kids.nationalgeographic.com/books/article/could-a-robot-become-president

National Geographic Kids: The Moon Landing
https://kids.nationalgeographic.com/history/article/moon-landing

Olson, Elsie. *AI Basics*. Minneapolis: Lerner Publications, 2025.

Index

Photo Acknowledgments

Image credits: Bettmann/Getty Images, pp. 4, 10; AP Photo/Neil A. Armstrong/NASA, p. 5; AP Photo, p. 6; Paul Quezada-Neiman/Alamy, p. 7; Evening Standard/Stringer/Getty Images, p. 8; The Washington Post/Getty Images, pp. 9, 13; Luis Alvarez/Getty Images, p. 11; Rokas Tenys/Alamy, p. 12; Drazen_/Getty Images, p. 14; AP Photo/Northrop Grumman/NASA, p. 15; M4OS Photos/Alamy, p. 16; Imaginechina Limited/Alamy, p. 17; Oscar Wong/Getty Images, p. 18; MDV Edwards/Shutterstock, p. 19; Eurasia Sport Images/Getty Images, p. 20; Wikimedia Commons PD, p. 21; FreshSplash/Getty Images, p. 22; MoMo Productions/Getty Images, p. 23; Sueddeutsche Zeitung Photo/Alamy, p. 24; LordHenriVoton/Getty Images, p. 25; Andrey_Popov/Shutterstock, p. 26; AP Photo/Gillian Flaccus, p. 27; John D. Ivanko/Alamy, p. 28; The White House, p. 29. Design elements: filo/Getty Images; JakeOlimb/Getty Images.

Cover: SEAN GLADWELL/Getty Images.